D1446170

CL

# GOD'S
# ALPHABET
# BOOK

# GOD'S ALPHABET BOOK

**Written by Brenda Eubanks**
**Illustrated by Tony Eubanks**

Loyola Press

**Chicago**

Dedicated to our three wonderful daughters
Ginny, Robyn, Rebecca

©1997  Text by Brenda Eubanks
Illustrations by Tony Eubanks

Printed in the United States of America

Loyola Press
3441 North Ashland Avenue
Chicago, Illinois 60657

Library of Congress Cataloging-in-Publication Data
Eubanks, Brenda.
God's alphabet book / written by Brenda Eubanks; illustrated by Tony Eubanks.
        p.   cm.
    Summary: Presents illustrations and scripture references for each letter of the alphabet, from A for Adam to Z for Zion.
    ISBN 0-8294-0968-8 (alk. paper)
    1. Bible—Juvenile literature. 2. English language—Alphabet—Juvenile literature. [1. Bible. 2. Alphabet.]
I. Eubanks, Tony, ill.  II. Title.
BS539.E93  1997
220.9'505–dc21
[E]
                                                                                97-16410
                                                                                     CIP
                                                                                      AC

97 98 99 00 01 / 10 9 8 7 6 5 4 3 2 1

is for Adam,
the first person God made.

Genesis 2:7

**B** is for Bethlehem,
where Baby Jesus was laid.

Luke 2:4−7

C is for Creation,
when God made the world.

Genesis 1:1

**D** is for David,
whose slingshot was hurled.

1 Samuel 17:49–50

E is for Egypt,
where Joseph was led.

Genesis 37:28

F is for Fish,
when thousands were fed.

Matthew 14:19–21

G is for Gabriel,
an angel of grace.

Luke 1:19

**H** is for Heaven,
a most perfect place.

Revelation 21:1–2

is for Isaac,
with Rebekah his wife.

Genesis 24:67

**J** is for Jonah,
  when the whale saved his life.

Jonah 1:17

is for Kindness,
a Samaritan's deed.

Luke 10:33–34

 is for Lions
that Daniel could feed.

Daniel 6:19–22

is for Magi,
the kings of the east.

Matthew 2:1–2

**N** is for Noah,
who saved all the beasts.

Genesis 6:19–20

is for Olives,
that grow on the hill.

Luke 19:37

**P** is for Prayer,
when we all seek God's will.

Matthew 21:22

is for Queen,
young Esther so true.

Esther 7:3

**R** is for Rainbow,
way up in the blue.

Genesis 9:13

is for Sarah,
a mother so old.

Genesis 21:2–3

T is for Temple,
where Jesus was bold.

John 2:14–16

**U** is for Universe,
and space without end.

Genesis 1:14–16

is for Vineyard,
which Naboth did tend.

I Kings 21:1

**W** is for Walls
of Jericho town.

Joshua 6:2–5

is for Xerxes,
a king of renown.

Ezra 4:6

is for Yellow,
God's sun in the sky.

Psalm 136:1–9

**Z** is for Zion,
God's mountain so high.

Psalm 48:1–2

And now that you've read about God's alphabet,
Lay yourself down, no longer to fret.
Dream your sweet dreams, and know in your heart,
That God will be near, and never apart.